5 Ingredient Cookbook: Fast and Easy]
Ingredients Inspired by The Med

by **Alissa Noel Grey**
Text copyright(c)2016 Alissa Noel Grey

Table Of Contents

No More Complicated Recipes

We just love the cozy feeling of sitting down with our family to a home-cooked dinner! But we also live in an age when we are constantly on the move and putting a home-cooked meal on the table during a busy weeknight looks like an impossible endeavor. In my new cookbook I have gathered the very best of my easy, five ingredient family recipes for evening meals, inspired by my Mediterranean origins, and prepared using simple and easy to find ingredients and a variety of cooking methods.

A delicious meal doesn't require tons of ingredients. All my recipes have a few things in common - they are healthy, they are family-friendly, and they can be prepared even by an inexperienced cook. Preparing meals at home may seem hard at the beginning but it soon turns out to be an amazingly rewarding experience. Cooking at home allows you to control the ingredients in your food, so you can choose natural ingredients instead of unhealthy processed foods. It also helps control the amount of salt and oils you use in your recipes.

The Mediterranean diet is not actually a "diet." Yes, it will help you lose weight and improve your health but it is really more of a relaxed and family-oriented lifestyle. It is living, cooking and eating with enthusiasm and love. People who live in the Mediterranean countries like Greece, Spain, France, Italy, Turkey and Morocco eat mainly local, everyday products that can be bought around the corner or grown in their own backyard. The Mediterranean way of cooking is in reality healthy home cooking embracing a variety of fresh ingredients such as whole grains, healthy fats, more colorful vegetables and fish, and less meat, and using wine, olive oil and fragrant herbs to create rich flavors.

A hallmark of Mediterranean dishes is that they derive deep flavor from simple ingredients prepared simply. Unlike many diets that involve increasing your intake of certain vitamins and minerals, with the Mediterranean diet you can always improvise, invent, vary recipes, and substitute one ingredient for another. It allows you to eat a wide variety of healthy whole foods in moderation, is high in good fats and dietary fiber and extremely low in saturated fats and bad cholesterol.

The Mediterranean diet will help you:

- Eat a well-balanced diet of whole natural foods
- Prevent heart disease, diabetes, arthritis, Alzheimer's, Parkinson's and cancer
- Lower cholesterol levels and blood pressure
- Improve cardiovascular health
- Improve brain and eye health
- Eat foods that are high in good fats and dietary fiber
- Lose weight
- Increase energy

Just remember these rules to be certain that you are really following a Mediterranean diet:

- Eat vegetables with every meal and eat fresh fruit every day;
- Use olive oil when cooking. Use little or no butter at all;
- Include at least two legume meals per week – add lentils, chickpeas or beans to salads, soups or casseroles.
- Include at least two servings of fish per week: oily fish, if possible, such salmon, mackerel, gem-fish, canned sardines and canned salmon;
- Eat smaller portions of lean meat – mainly chicken, lamb, and beef;
- Eat yogurt and cheese in moderation;
- Consume wine in moderation, only with meals;
- Eat nuts, seeds, fresh fruit and dried fruit as snacks and dessert;

Caprese Salad

Serves: 5-6

Prep time: 4 min

Ingredients:

3-4 tomatoes, sliced

7 oz mozzarella cheese, sliced

6-7 fresh basil leaves

3 tbsp extra virgin olive oil

2 tbsp red wine vinegar

Directions:

Slice the tomatoes and mozzarella, then layer the tomato slices, whole fresh basil leaves and mozzarella slices on a plate.

Drizzle olive oil and vinegar over the salad and serve.

Chicken and Broccoli Salad

Serves: 4

Prep time: 10 min

Ingredients:

2 cooked chicken breasts, diced

1 small head broccoli, cut into florets

1 cup cherry tomatoes, halved

2 tbsp olive oil

2 tbsp basil pesto

Directions:

Heat two tablespoons of olive oil in a non-stick frying pan and gently sauté broccoli for 5-6 minutes until tender.

Place broccoli in a large salad bowl. Stir in the chicken and tomatoes. Add the basil pesto, toss to combine and serve.

Summer Pasta Salad

Serves 4

Prep time: 25 min

Ingredients:

2 cups small pasta

2 hard boiled eggs, peeled and diced

1 cup ham, diced

10 gherkins, diced

1/2 cup mayonnaise

Directions:

Cook pasta as directed on package. When cooked through but al dente, remove from heat, drain and rinse.

Combine the ham, pasta and all other ingredients. Stir, refrigerate for 30 minutes, and serve.

Vitamin Chicken Salad

Serves: 4

Prep time: 5 min

Ingredients:

3 cooked chicken breasts, shredded

2 yellow bell peppers, thinly sliced

1/2 red onion, thinly sliced

1 large green apple, peeled and thinly sliced

2 tbsp light mustard

Directions:

In a deep salad bowl, combine the onion, peppers, apple and chicken.

Stir in the mustard, refrigerate for 10 minutes, and serve.

Mashed Avocado and Chicken Salad

Serves: 4-5

Prep time: 5 min

Ingredients:

2 cooked chicken breasts, diced

1 small red onion, finely chopped

2 ripe avocados, mashed with a fork

2 tbsp olive paste

Directions:

Place the chicken in a medium sized salad bowl.

In a plate, mash the avocados using either a fork or a potato masher and add them to the chicken. Add in the onion and olive paste. Stir to combine and serve.

Superfood Macaroni and Beet Salad

Serves 4

Prep time 25 min

Ingredients:

2 cups macaroni

4 oz smoked salmon

1 cup roasted walnuts

2 boiled beets, peeled and diced

1 cup mayonnaise

Directions:

Cook macaroni as directed on package. When cooked through but al dente, remove from heat, drain and rinse.

Combine the macaroni, mayonnaise, salmon, walnuts and beets. Refrigerate for 10 minutes and serve.

Pea and Orzo Salad

Serves 4

Prep time 25 min

Ingredients:

1 cup orzo

2 cups frozen peas

1 cup finely cut parsley leaves

1-2 spring onions, finely cut

4 tbsp basil pesto

Directions:

Cook orzo in a large saucepan of boiling, salted water, following packet directions until tender. Add peas in the last 3 minutes of cooking. Drain well and return to pot.

Add pesto to the orzo mixture. Stir in parsley and serve.

Strained Yogurt Salad

Serves: 4

Prep time 25 min

Ingredients:

4-5 large pickled cucumbers, diced

4 cups of plain yogurt

½ cup crushed walnuts

2 garlic cloves, crushed

1/2 cup dill, finely cut

Directions:

Strain the yogurt in a piece of cheesecloth or a clean white dishtowel.

Dice the pickled cucumbers and place them in a deep bowl. Add the crushed walnuts, garlic, and the finely chopped dill.

Stir in the drained yogurt, refrigerate for at least 20 minutes and serve.

Potato Salad

Serves 4

Prep time: 30 min

Ingredients:

4-5 large potatoes

2-3 leeks, white parts only, very finely chopped

juice of ½ a lemon

5 tbsp extra virgin olive oil

salt and pepper, to taste

Directions:

Peel and boil the potatoes for about 25 minutes, leave to cool and dice.

In a salad bowl add the leeks, lemon juice, salt, pepper and olive oil. Stir to combine. Add in the potatoes, toss to combine and serve.

Avocado and Corn Salad

Serves: 4

Prep time: 5 min

Ingredients:

2 avocados, peeled and finely chopped

1 can corn kernels, drained

4-5 green onions, finely chopped

3 tbsp lemon juice

½ tsp cumin

Directions:

Combine avocados, corn, onions, cumin and lemon juice in a salad bowl and serve immediately.

Avocado, Black Bean and Red Pepper Salad

Serves: 4-5

Prep time: 6-7 min

Ingredients:

2 avocados, peeled and diced

1 can black beans, drained

2 red bell pepper, diced

1-2 green onions, finely chopped

3 tbsp lemon juice

Directions:

Place avocados, beans, bell peppers, green onions, garlic, coriander and cumin in a salad bowl.

Sprinkle with lemon juice and olive oil, toss to combine and serve immediately.

Avocado and Roasted Balsamic Mushroom Salad

Serves: 4

Prep time: 20 min

Ingredients:

10-15 mushrooms, halved

2 tbsp balsamic vinegar

3 tbsp extra virgin olive oil

1 avocado, peeled and sliced

1/2 cup parsley leaves, finely cut

Directions:

Line a baking tray with baking paper and place the mushrooms on it. Drizzle with olive oil and balsamic vinegar.

Roast in a preheated to 375 F oven for 15 minutes, or until golden and tender.

Combine the avocado and mushrooms in a salad bowl. Stir in parsley. Drizzle some more balsamic vinegar and olive oil if desired.

Roasted Peppers with Garlic and Parsley

Serves 4-6

Prep time: 15 min

Ingredients:

2 lbs green bell peppers

3-4 cloves garlic, chopped

1/2 cup fresh parsley, finely cut

4-5 tbsp extra virgin oil

4 tbsp white wine vinegar

Directions:

Roast the peppers in the oven at 480 F until the skins are a little burnt. Place them in a brown paper bag or a lidded container and leave them covered for about 10 minutes. Peel the skins and remove the seeds.

Cut the peppers into 1 inch strips lengthwise and layer them in a salad bowl. Mix together the oil, vinegar, salt and pepper, chopped garlic and the chopped parsley leaves. Pour over the peppers. Serve chilled.

Feta Cheese Stuffed Tomatoes

Serves 4

Prep time: 5 min

Ingredients:

4 large ripe tomatoes

2 cups feta cheese, crumbled

1 cup finely cut parsley

1 tsp paprika

2 tbsp extra virgin olive oil

Directions:

Cut the top of each tomato in such a way as to be able to stuff the tomato and cover with the cap. Scoop out the seeds and central part of the tomatoes to create a hollow.

Mash the scooped out tomato parts with a fork, add to the feta cheese and stir to make a homogeneous mixture. Add in the olive oil, paprika and parsley. Stuff the tomatoes with the cheese mixture and cover with the caps. Serve chilled.

Avocado and Cucumber Salad

Serves: 4-5

Prep time: 10 min

Ingredients:

2 avocados, peeled, halved and sliced

½ red onion, thinly sliced

1 large cucumber, halved, sliced

3 tbsp basil pesto

2 tbsp lemon juice

Directions:

Combine the avocados, onion and cucumber in a bowl. Stir in the basil pesto and serve.

Italian Grilled Cheese Sandwich

Serves: 4

Prep time: 5 min

Ingredients:

2 eggs

2 tbsp milk

3 tablespoons grated Parmesan cheese

4 slices American cheese

8 slices white bread

Directions:

Whisk eggs, milk and Parmesan cheese together in a bowl. Place each American cheese slice between two pieces of bread to assemble 4 sandwiches. Dip both sides of each sandwich in egg mixture.

Heat a non-stick frying pan over medium heat. Place sandwiches in the hot frying pan and cook until golden brown and cheese is melted, 2-3 minutes per side.

Radish and Goat Cheese Toast

Serves: 4

Prep time: 5 min

Ingredients:

4 slices crusty bread

4 oz creamy goat cheese

8 large radishes, thinly sliced

2 tbsp chopped fresh mint

salt, to taste

Directions:

Toast the bread until golden. Spread with goat cheese and top with fresh mint and radishes. Season with salt to taste and serve.

Avocado and Feta Toast with Pomegranate Seeds

Serves: 4

Prep time: 5 min

Ingredients:

1 avocado, peeled and chopped

½ cup feta cheese, crumbled

4 thick slices white bread, lightly toasted

1 cup pomegranate seeds

Directions:

Mash the avocado and feta with a fork until smooth.

Toast 4 slices of white bread until golden. Spoon 1/4 of the avocado mixture onto each slice of bread. Top with pomegranate seeds and serve.

Avocado and Olive Paste on Toasted Rye Bread

Serves: 4

Prep time: 5 min

Ingredients:

1 avocado, halved, peeled and finely chopped

1 tbsp green onions, finely chopped

2 tbsp green olive paste

1 tbsp lemon juice

Directions:

Mash avocado with a fork or potato masher until almost smooth. Add the onions, green olive paste and lemon juice. Season with salt and pepper to taste. Stir to combine.

Toast 4 slices of rye bread until golden. Spoon 1/4 of the avocado mixture onto each slice of bread.

Breakfast Feta Sandwiches

Serves: 4

Prep time: 3-4 min

Ingredients:

4 slices white bread

1 cup crumbled feta cheese

1 tbsp finely cut dill

1 tomato, thinly sliced

salt, to taste

Directions:

Mash the feta and dill with a fork until smooth.

Spread this mixture on the four slices of bread. Top each slice with 4 tomato slices and serve.

Turkey Sausage, Tomato and Cheese Sandwiches

Serves: 4

Prep time: 7-8 min

Ingredients:

4 thick turkey sausages

8 slices white bread

1/4 cup tomato sauce

1 1/2 cups shredded iceberg lettuce

4 slices Swiss cheese

Directions:

Heat a non-stick frying pan over medium-high heat. Add sausages and cook, turning, for 4-5 minutes or until cooked through. Thinly slice.

Spread tomato sauce over 4 slices of bread. Add iceberg lettuce, cheese and the sausage. Top with remaining bread, cut in half and serve.

Avocado, Roast Beef and Lettuce Sandwiches

Serves: 2

Prep time: 3-4 min

Ingredients:

4 slices rye bread

4 oz quality roast beef, thinly sliced

1/2 avocado, peeled and sliced

2 large leaves lettuce

1/2 tomato, thinly sliced

Directions:

Layer two slices of bread with roast beef, one lettuce leaf, two slices tomato and two slices avocado.

Top with remaining bread slices and serve.

Hot Ham, Cheese and Jalapeño Sandwiches

Serves: 2

Prep time: 20 min

Ingredients:

2 poppyseed buns

8 oz thinly sliced ham

8 oz thinly sliced Swiss cheese

2 tbsp butter

1/2 cup pickled jalapeños

Directions:

Cut buns in half and spread butter on each side. Evenly divide the ham and cheese among the buns.

Add jalapeños to the tops of the ham-cheese buns, then top each sandwich with their reserved bun caps.

Preheat oven to 325 F. Wrap each sandwich in foil, place them on a baking sheet, and bake for 15 minutes, or until cheese has melted and the sandwich is heated through.

Carrot, Sprouts and Raisin Sandwiches

Serves: 2

Prep time: 3-4 min

Ingredients:

4 slices whole wheat bread

1/2 cup spreadable cream cheese

3 tbsp honey

1 cup Alfalfa sprouts

Directions:

Spread 2 slices bread with cream cheese. Drizzle over honey and spread carrots and alfalfa sprouts.

Top with the rest of the bread and cut in half.

Leek, Brown Rice and Potato Soup

Serves: 4-5

Prep time: 35 min

Ingredients:

3 potatoes, peeled and diced

2 leeks, finely chopped

1/4 cup brown rice

5 cups water

3 tbsp extra virgin olive oil

Directions:

Heat olive oil in a deep soup pot and sauté leeks for 3-4 minutes. Add in potatoes and cook for a minute more. Stir in water, bring to a boil, and add the brown rice.

Reduce heat and simmer for 30 minutes.

Farfalle with Watercress, Cherry Tomatoes, and Feta

Serves 6

Prep time: 20 min

Ingredients:

8 oz farfale pasta

1 cup crumbled feta cheese

2 cups cherry tomatoes, halved

3 cups watercress leaves

1 cup black olives, pitted

salt and pepper, to taste

Directions:

Prepare pasta as described on package directions. Place the tomatoes in a colander and drain the pasta over them for a super-quick blanch.

Place the cheese in a large bowl; top with the watercress, tomatoes, pasta and olives. Season with salt and pepper to taste, toss to combine, and serve.

Pasta alla Genovese

Serves: 4-5

Prep time: 30 min

Ingredients:

12 oz small pasta

1-2 medium potatoes, peeled and cut roughly into chunks

4 oz green beans, trimmed

5-6 tbsp pesto

Parmesan cheese, to serve

Directions:

Prepare the pasta according to package directions.

Cook the potatoes in boiling, salted water until tender, adding the green beans for the last 3-4 minutes of cooking.

Drain the pasta. Drain the beans and potatoes then tip into the pasta together with the pesto and a squeeze of lemon. Toss everything to combine and serve with extra Parmesan.

Ground Beef and Brussels Sprouts

Serves: 4

Prep time: 20 min

Ingredients:

6 oz ground beef

3 garlic cloves, crushed

½ cup grated sweet potato

1 cup grated Brussels sprouts

1 tbsp extra virgin olive oil

Directions:

In a medium saucepan, heat the olive oil over medium heat. Gently sauté the ground beef and garlic until just fragrant. Add in the sweet potato and cook until the meat is fully cooked.

Stir in the Brussels sprouts and cook for about 5 minutes more. Season with salt and pepper to taste and serve.

Italian Mini Meatballs

Serves: 6

Prep time: 35 min

Ingredients:

1 lb ground beef

1 onion, grated

1 egg, lightly whisked

2 tbsp Italian seasoning

2 tbsp olive oil

Directions:

Combine ground beef, oil, onion, egg and Italian seasoning. Mix very well with hands. Roll tablespoonfuls of the meat mixture into balls.

Place meatballs on a lined baking tray. Bake 20 minutes or until brown. Transfer to a serving plate and serve.

Steak with Olives and Mushrooms

Serves: 6

Prep time: 20 min

Ingredients:

1 lb boneless beef sirloin steak, 3/4-inch thick, cut into 4 pieces

1 large onion, sliced

5-6 white button mushrooms

1/2 cup green olives, coarsely chopped

4 tbsp extra virgin olive oil

Directions:

Heat olive oil in a heavy bottomed skillet over medium-high heat. Cook the steaks until well browned on both sides then set aside in a plate.

Gently sauté the onion in the same skillet, for 2-3 minutes, stirring occasionally. Add in the mushrooms and olives and cook until the mushrooms are done.

Return the steaks to the skillet, cover, cook for 5-6 minutes and serve.

Spicy Mustard Chicken

Serves: 4

Prep time: 65 min

Ingredients:

4 chicken breasts

2 garlic cloves, crushed

1/3 cup chicken broth

3 tbsp Dijon mustard

1 tsp chili powder

Directions:

In a small bowl, mix the mustard, chicken broth, garlic and chili. Marinate the chicken for 30 minutes.

Bake in a preheated to 375 F oven for 35 minutes.

Walnut and Oregano Crusted Chicken

Serves: 4

Prep time: 35-40 min

Ingredients:

4 skinless, boneless chicken breasts

10-12 fresh oregano leaves

1/2 cup walnuts, chopped

2 garlic cloves, chopped

2 eggs, beaten

Directions:

Blend the garlic, oregano and walnuts in a food processor until a rough crumb is formed. Place this mixture on a plate.

Whisk eggs in a deep bowl. Dip each chicken breast in the beaten egg then roll it in the walnut mixture. Place coated chicken on a baking tray and bake at 375 F for 13 minutes each side.

Chicken and Onion Casserole

Serves: 4

Prep time: 35 min

Ingredients:

4 chicken breasts

4-5 large onions, sliced

2 leeks, cut

1 cup black olives, pitted

4 tbsp extra virgin olive oil

Directions:

Heat olive oil in a large, deep frying pan over medium-high heat. Brown chicken, turning, for 2-3 minutes each side or until golden. Set aside in a casserole dish.

Cut the onions and leeks and add them on and around the chicken, Add in olives, thyme, salt and black pepper to taste. Cover with a lid or aluminum foil and bake at 375 F for 35 minutes, or until the chicken is cooked through. Uncover and return to the oven for 5 minutes or until chicken is crispy.

Chicken and Mushrooms

Serves: 4

Prep time: 20-30 min

Ingredients:

4 chicken breasts, diced

2 lbs mushrooms, chopped

1 onion, chopped

4 tbsp extra virgin olive oil

salt and black, pepper to taste

Directions:

Heat olive oil in a deep frying pan over medium-high heat. Brown chicken, stirring, for 2 minutes each side, or until golden.

Add the chopped onion, mushrooms, salt and black pepper, and stir to combine.

Reduce heat, cover and simmer for 30 minutes. Uncover and simmer for 5 more minutes.

Blue Cheese and Mushroom Chicken

Serves 4

Prep time: 25 min

Ingredients:

4 chicken breast halves

1 cup crumbled blue cheese

1 cup sour cream

salt and black pepper, to taste

1/2 cup parsley, finely cut

Directions:

Heat the oven to 350 degrees F. Spray a casserole with non stick spray. Place all ingredients into it, turn chicken to coat.

Bake for 20 minutes or until chicken juices run clear. Sprinkle with parsley and serve.

Herb-Roasted Lamb Leg

Serves 4

Prep time: 130 min

Ingredients:

1 (6-lb) boneless leg of lamb, trimmed

2 cups fresh spinach leaves

1/3 cup water

2 tbsp Italian seasoning

4 tbsp extra virgin olive oil

Directions:

Combine spinach, Italian seasoning and olive oil in a food processor. Process until finely minced.

Thoroughly coat the top and sides of the lamb with this mixture.

Place in the bottom of a large roasting pan. Add water and cook, covered, at 300 F for approximately two hours or until cooked through.

Uncover and cook for 10 minutes more.

Spring Lamb Stew

Serves 4

Prep time: 30-40 min

Ingredients:

1 lb lamb, cubed

1 lb white mushrooms, chopped

4 cups fresh spring onions, chopped

3 tbsp extra virgin olive oil

1 tbsp Italian seasoning

Directions:

Heat olive oil in a deep casserole. Gently brown lamb pieces for 2-3 minutes. Add in the mushrooms and cook for a minute more, stirring.

Stir in Italian seasoning, cover, and cook for an hour or until tender. Add in spring onions and simmer for 10 minutes more.

Uncover and cook until almost all the liquid evaporates.

Pork and Mushroom Crock Pot

Serves 4

Prep time:7-9 hours

Ingredients:

2 lbs pork tenderloin, sliced

1 lb chopped white button mushrooms

1 can cream of mushroom soup

1 cup sour cream

salt and black pepper, to taste

Directions:

Spray the slow cooker with non stick spray.

Combine all ingredients into the slow cooker.

Cover, and cook on low for 7-9 hours.

Slow Cooked Pot Roast

Serves: 4

Prep time: 8-10 hours

Ingredients:

2 lb pot roast

1-2 garlic cloves, crushed

1 small onion, finely cut

1/2 cup chicken broth

2 tbsp Italian seasoning

Directions:

Spray the slow cooker with non stick spray.

Place the roast in the slow cooker.

In a bowl, combine the chicken broth, garlic, onions and Italian seasoning. Spread this sauce over the meat.

Cover and cook on low 8-10 hours.

Balsamic Roasted Carrots and Baby Onions

Serves: 4

Prep time: 50 min

Ingredients:

2 bunches baby carrots, scrubbed, ends trimmed

10 small onions, peeled, halved

4 tbsp 100% pure maple syrup (unprocessed)

1 tsp thyme

2 tbsp extra virgin olive oil

Directions:

Preheat oven to 350F. Line a baking tray with baking paper.

Place the carrots, onion, thyme and oil in a large bowl and toss until well coated. Arrange carrots and onion, in a single layer, on the baking tray. Roast for 25 minutes or until tender.

Sprinkle over the maple syrup and vinegar and toss to coat. Roast for 25-30 minutes more or until vegetables are tender and caramelized. Season with salt and pepper to taste and serve.

Baked Cauliflower

Serves: 4

Prep time: 25 min

Ingredients:

1 small cauliflower, cut into florets

1 tbsp garlic powder

1 tsp paprika

4 tbsp extra virgin olive oil

grated Parmesan cheese, to taste

Directions:

Combine olive oil, paprika and garlic powder together. Toss in the cauliflower florets and place in a baking dish in one layer.

Bake in a preheated to 350 F oven for 20 minutes. Take out of the oven, stir, and sprinkle with Parmesan cheese. Bake for 5 minutes more or until golden.

Baked Bean and Rice Casserole

Serves: 4

Prep time: 30 min

Ingredients:

1 can red beans, rinsed

1 cup water

2/3 cup rice

2 onions, chopped

2 tsp dried mint

Directions:

Heat olive oil in an ovenproof casserole dish and gently sauté the chopped onions for 1-2 minutes. Stir in the rice and cook, stirring constantly, for another minute.

Rinse the beans and add them to the casserole. Stir in a cup of water and the mint and bake in a preheated to 350 F oven for 20 minutes.

Okra and Tomato Casserole

Serves: 4

Prep time: 25 min

Ingredients:

1 lb okra, trimmed

3 tomatoes, cut into wedges

3 garlic cloves, chopped

1 cup fresh parsley leaves, finely cut

3 tbsp extra virgin olive oil

Directions:

In a deep ovenproof baking dish, combine okra, sliced tomatoes, olive oil and garlic.

Toss to combine and bake in a preheated to 350 F oven for 45 minutes, or until the okra is tender. Sprinkle with parsley and serve.

Spicy Baked Feta with Tomatoes

Serves: 4

Prep time: 15 min

Ingredients:

1 lb feta cheese, cut in slices

2 ripe tomatoes, sliced

1 onion, sliced

3 tbsp extra virgin olive oil

1/2 tbsp hot paprika

Directions:

Preheat the oven to 430F

In an ovenproof baking dish, arrange the slices of onions and tomatoes overlapping slightly but not too much. Sprinkle with olive oil.

Bake for 5 minutes then place the feta slices on top of the vegetables. Sprinkle with hot paprika. Bake for 15 more minutes and serve.

Feta Cheese Baked in Foil

Serves: 4

Prep time: 15 min

Ingredients:

14 oz feta cheese, cut in slices

4 oz butter

1 tbsp paprika

1 tsp dried oregano

aluminum foil, enough to cover 4 slices of cheese

Directions:

Cut the cheese into four medium-thick slices and place on sheets of butter lined aluminum foil.

Place a little bit of butter on top each feta cheese piece, sprinkle with paprika and dried oregano and wrap. Place on a tray and bake in a preheated to 350 F oven for 15 minutes.

Salmon and Spinach with Feta Cheese

Serves: 4

Prep time: 15 min

Ingredients:

4 salmon fillets, skin on

1 bag frozen spinach

4-5 green onions, chopped

1 cup crumbled feta cheese

4 tbsp extra virgin olive oil

Directions:

In a skillet, heat olive oil on medium-high. Cook the spinach and the green onions for 2-3 min, stirring once or twice. Add in the feta cheese. Cook for 1 minute more.

Place salmon skin side down in a single layer on a lined baking tray and roast for 10-12 minutes or until it is cooked through and flakes easily with a fork.

Spoon the spinach mixture onto plates, then top with the salmon and serve with lemon wedges.

Almond and Oregano Crusted Fish Fillets

Serves: 4

Prep time: 10 min

Ingredients:

4 white fish fillets

1 tsp dried oregano

1/2 cup raw almonds, chopped

2 tbsp grated Parmesan cheese

3 egg whites, beaten

Directions:

Blend the Parmesan cheese, oregano and almonds in a food processor until a light crumb is formed. Place on a plate.

Whisk egg whites in a deep bowl. Dip each fish fillet in the beaten egg whites then roll it in the almond mixture.

Place coated fish on a lined baking tray and bake at 375 F for 6-7 minutes each side.

Salmon Kebabs

Serves: 4-5

Prep time: 30 min

Ingredients:

2 shallots, ends trimmed, halved

2 zucchinis, cut in 2 inch cubes

1 cup cherry tomatoes

6 skinless salmon fillets, cut into 1 inch pieces

Directions:

Preheat barbecue or char grill on medium-high. Thread fish cubes onto skewers, then zucchinis, shallots and tomatoes. Repeat to make 12 kebabs.

Bake the kebabs for about 3 minutes each side for medium cooked.

Transfer to a plate, cover with foil and set aside for 5 minutes to rest.

Mediterranean Baked Salmon

Serves: 4-5

Prep time: 35 min

Ingredients:

2 (6 oz) boneless salmon fillets

1 onion, thinly sliced

3 tbsp olive oil

1 tbsp Italian seasoning

3 tbsp Parmesan cheese

Directions:

Preheat oven to 350 F. Place the salmon fillets in a baking dish, sprinkle with the Italian seasoning, top with onion, drizzle with olive oil and sprinkle with Parmesan cheese.

Cover the dish with foil and bake for 30 minutes, or until the fish flakes easily.

Feta and Tomato Scrambled Eggs

Serves 4

Prep time: 10 min

Ingredients:

5-6 green onions, finely cut

10 oz feta cheese, crumbled

1 cup diced tomatoes

8 eggs, whisked

2 tbsp olive oil

Directions:

In a large pan, sauté the onions and tomatoes in olive oil, over medium heat, until soft, about 2 min.

Add in the feta cheese and whisked eggs, stir, and cook until well mixed and not too liquid.

Set aside for 3-4 minutes, and serve.

FREE BONUS RECIPES: 20 Superfood Paleo and Vegan Smoothies for Vibrant Health and Easy Weight Loss

Kale and Kiwi Smoothie

Serves: 2

Prep time: 2-3 min

Ingredients:

2-3 ice cubes

1 cup orange juice

1 small pear, peeled and chopped

2 kiwi, peeled and chopped

2-3 kale leaves

2-3 dates, pitted

Directions:

Combine all ingredients in a high speed blender and blend until smooth.

Delicious Broccoli Smoothie

Serves: 2

Prep time: 2-3 min

Ingredients:

2-3 frozen broccoli florets

1 cup coconut milk

1 banana, peeled and chopped

1 cup pineapple, cut

1 peach, chopped

1 tsp cinnamon

Directions:

Combine all ingredients in a high speed blender and blend until smooth.

Papaya Smoothie

Serves: 2

Prep time: 2-3 min

Ingredients:

2-3 frozen broccoli florets

1 cup orange juice

1 small ripe avocado, peeled, cored and diced

1 cup papaya

1 cup fresh strawberries

Directions:

Combine all ingredients in a high speed blender and blend until smooth.

Beet and Papaya Smoothie

Serves: 2

Prep time: 2-3 min

Ingredients:

3-4 ice cubes

1 cup orange juice

1 banana, peeled and chopped

1 cup papaya

1 small beet, peeled and cut

Directions:

Combine all ingredients in a high speed blender and blend until smooth.

Lean Green Smoothie

Serves: 2

Prep time: 2-3 min

Ingredients:

1 frozen banana, chopped

1 cup orange juice

2-3 kale leaves, stems removed

1 small cucumber, peeled and chopped

1/2 cup fresh parsley leaves

½ tsp grated ginger

Directions:

Combine all ingredients in a high speed blender and blend until smooth.

Easy Antioxidant Smoothie

Serves: 2

Prep time: 2-3 min

Ingredients:

2-3 frozen broccoli florets

1 cup orange juice

2 plums, cut

1 cup raspberries

1 tsp ginger powder

Directions:

Combine all ingredients in a high speed blender and blend until smooth.

Healthy Purple Smoothie

Serves: 2

Prep time: 2-3 min

Ingredients:

2-3 frozen broccoli florets

1 cup water

1/2 avocado, peeled and chopped

3 plums, chopped

1 cup blueberries

Directions:

Combine all ingredients in a high speed blender and blend until smooth.

Mom's Favorite Kale Smoothie

Serves: 2

Prep time: 2-3 min

Ingredients:

2-3 ice cubes

1½ cup orange juice

1 green small apple, cut

½ cucumber, chopped

2-3 leaves kale

½ cup raspberries

Directions:

Combine all ingredients in a high speed blender and blend until smooth.

Creamy Green Smoothie

Serves: 2

Prep time: 2-3 min

Ingredients:

1 frozen banana

1 cup coconut milk

1 small pear, chopped

1 cup baby spinach

1 cup grapes

1 tbsp coconut butter

1 tsp vanilla extract

Directions:

Combine all ingredients in a high speed blender and blend until smooth.

Strawberry and Arugula Smoothie

Serves: 2

Prep time: 2-3 min

Ingredients:

2 cups frozen strawberries

1 cup unsweetened almond milk

10-12 arugula leaves

1/2 tsp ground cinnamon

Directions:

Combine ice, almond milk, strawberries, arugula and cinnamon in a high speed blender. Blend until smooth and serve.

Emma's Amazing Smoothie

Serves: 2

Prep time: 2-3 min

Ingredients:

1 frozen banana, chopped

1 cup orange juice

1 large nectarine, sliced

1/2 zucchini, peeled and chopped

2-3 dates, pitted

Directions:

Combine all ingredients in a high speed blender and blend until smooth.

Good-To-Go Morning Smoothie

Serves: 2

Prep time: 2-3 min

Ingredients:

1 cup frozen strawberries

1 cup apple juice

1 banana, chopped

1 cup raw asparagus, chopped

1 tbsp ground flaxseed

Directions:

Combine all ingredients in a high speed blender and blend until smooth.

Endless Energy Smoothie

Serves: 2

Prep time: 2-3 min

Ingredients:

1 frozen banana, chopped

11/2 cup green tea

1 cup chopped pineapple

2 raw asparagus spears, chopped

1 lime, juiced

1 tbsp chia seeds

Directions:

Combine all ingredients in a high speed blender and blend until smooth.

High-fibre Fruit Smoothie

Serves: 2

Prep time: 2-3 min

Ingredients:

1 frozen banana, chopped

1 cup orange juice

2 cups chopped papaya

1 cup shredded cabbage

1 tbsp chia seeds

Directions:

Combine all ingredients in a high speed blender and blend until smooth.

Nutritious Green Smoothie

Serves: 2

Prep time: 2-3 min

Ingredients:

2-3 frozen broccoli florets

1 cup apple juice

1 large pear, chopped

1 kiwi, peeled and chopped

1 cup spinach leaves

1-2 dates, pitted

Directions:

Combine all ingredients in a high speed blender and blend until smooth.

Apricot, Strawberry and Banana Smoothie

Serves: 2

Prep time: 2-3 min

Ingredients:

1 frozen banana

11/2 cup almond milk

5 dried apricots

1 cup fresh strawberries

Directions:

Combine all ingredients in a high speed blender and blend until smooth.

Spinach and Green Apple Smoothie

Serves: 2

Prep time: 2-3 min

Ingredients:

3-4 ice cubes

1 cup unsweetened almond milk

1 banana, peeled and chopped

2 green apples, peeled and chopped

1 cup raw spinach leaves

3-4 dates, pitted

1 tsp grated ginger

Directions:

Combine all ingredients in a high speed blender and blend until smooth.

Superfood Blueberry Smoothie

Serves: 2

Prep time: 2-3 min

Ingredients:

2-3 cubes frozen spinach

1 cup green tea

1 banana

2 cups blueberries

1 tbsp ground flaxseed

Directions:

Combine all ingredients in a high speed blender and blend until smooth.

Zucchini and Blueberry Smoothie

Serves: 2

Prep time: 2-3 min

Ingredients:

1 cup frozen blueberries

1 cup unsweetened almond milk

1 banana

1 zucchini, peeled and chopped

Directions:

Combine all ingredients in a high speed blender and blend until smooth.

Tropical Spinach Smoothie

Serves: 2

Prep time: 2-3 min

Ingredients:

1/2 cup crushed ice or 3-4 ice cubes

1 cup coconut milk

1 mango, peeled and diced

1 cup fresh spinach leaves

4-5 dates, pitted

1/2 tsp vanilla extract

Directions:

Combine all ingredients in a high speed blender and blend until smooth.

About the Author

Alissa Grey is a fitness and nutrition enthusiast who loves to teach people about losing weight and feeling better about themselves. She lives in a small French village in the foothills of a beautiful mountain range with her husband, three teenage kids, two free spirited dogs, and various other animals.

Alissa is incredibly lucky to be able to cook and eat natural foods, mostly grown nearby, something she's done since she was a teenager. She enjoys yoga, running, reading, hanging out with her family, and growing organic vegetables and herbs.

Printed in Great Britain
by Amazon